~~POCKET~~
ENCOURAGER
for *Women*

POCKET ENCOURAGER

for *Women*

Biblical Help for Difficult Times

By Selwyn Hughes
with contributions from
Dr Bill and Frances Munro
David and Maureen Brown
Helena Wilkinson
Hilary Vogel

*May our
Lord Jesus Christ himself
and God our Father,
who loved us and by his grace
gave us eternal encouragement
and good hope,
encourage your hearts
and strengthen you
in every good deed and word.*

2 Thessalonians 2:16–17

Pocket Encourager for Women

Copyright © CWR 2001
Reprinted 2001
ISBN 1 85345 178 9

Concept development, editing, design and production by CWR
Printed in England by Linney Print

Published by CWR, Waverley Abbey House, Waverley Lane,
Farnham, Surrey GU9 8EP

Contents

Everyone needs
Encouragement

From time to time we all need encouragement. In my role as a Christian counsellor I have met only a few people who didn't respond positively to a few carefully chosen and biblically-based words of encouragement. Some of the most remembered moments in my own life have been those when I have been overtaken by a pressing problem and someone has stimulated my faith with a God-given, reassuring word.

The word discourage means "to deprive of courage, to dishearten, to deter". Almost every day we face discouraging circumstances and situations: a put-down from someone, a critical word, plans that don't seem to work out, loneliness, sorrow, failure, doubts, and so on. The word encourage means "to inspire with new confidence and courage, to give spirit or hope, to hearten, to spur on, to give help." It is gratifying when we are caught up in the throes of discouragement to have a friend or relative say something (or do something) that is encouraging. But what do we do when such encouragement is not available?

That famous Old Testament character David was once in this situation. The incident is recorded for us in the First Book of Samuel chapters 27, 29 and 30. Fleeing for his life from King Saul, David offered his services, and those of his 600 men, to King Achish, a Philistine. And the king, accepting the offer, gave David and his men first Gath, then the city of Ziklag for their home. David, his men and their families settled there.

One day King Achish took his troops to join in a combined Philistine attack against Israel, and astonishingly, David and his soldiers went along with them to fight against their own people. But King Achish's colleagues refused to trust David and his men in a battle against their own, so they decided to send them back to Ziklag. On returning there they found that a group of desert raiders called the Amalekites had burned the city to the ground and had taken captive everyone they had found. David and his men, we read: "wept aloud until they had no strength left to weep" (1 Samuel 30:4).

To make matters worse, David's men turned on him and blamed him for their predicament. They even discussed among themselves the idea of stoning him: "each one was bitter in spirit because of his sons and daughters" (1 Samuel 30:6). In addition to the problems with his troops, David had to cope with the loss of his own family also. His state of distress was such that right there his career could easily have come to an end. Then we are introduced to one of the great "but's" of the Bible: "But David encouraged ... himself in the Lord his God" (v.6, Amplified Bible).

How did he do it? He would have prayed of course, and that is always important when dealing with discouragement. But I think he did something more – he recalled what he knew of God, and thought about what he had learned concerning the Almighty as a shepherd boy when he meditated upon Him in the Judean hills.

"The secret of recovering your footing spiritually," says Jim Packer, the well-known theologian, "lies in the little word *think.*" That was undoubtedly where David began; he made himself recall what he knew of God and applied it to his own situation at that moment. The Puritans used to call it "preaching to oneself". Every time we are discouraged, every time we reel under the blow of some traumatic experience, every time our feelings scream out in pain, we must assert the facts of our faith over our feelings. We can't wait for the unpleasant and uncomfortable feelings to subside; we must take control over the runaway feelings by reminding ourselves of what we know about God.

I imagine that David would have reminded himself of such facts as these: God is sovereign, God is love, God is forgiving, God is faithful, God is consistent, God is merciful. Dwelling on these thoughts would have brought great encouragement to David's heart. The consequence of all this was that he found the guidance he needed to restore the situation completely. Read the story for yourself in the rest of 1 Samuel 30.

Every Christian woman ought to know how to do what David did, and this pocketbook is an attempt to assist you in doing that. Friends are wonderful (thank God for them), but we must know how to think biblically about life's problems, to talk to ourselves about the facts of our faith and then find the appropriate scriptures that relate to our problem. It is imperative that we know what parts of the Bible to turn to in times of testing, and to know also how to talk ourselves into a new mood of optimism and faith. The things we tell ourselves greatly affect the way we feel – and this is why we must learn to fill our minds with the truths of God's eternal and unchanging Word.

I can't emphasise strongly enough that our negative self-talk is often responsible for the way we feel. We talk ourselves into a low mood by repeating statements to ourselves that either minimise or maximise the facts. And just as we talk ourselves into downcast feelings so we can talk ourselves out of them.

In this publication we have taken key issues addressed in the earlier CWR publication *Your Personal Encourager*, and added additional material written by people involved in the "ministry of encouragement" that is particularly relevant to women. If a particular problem that you are facing does not fall within these categories then look for the one that comes closest to it. I feel confident you will find something that will revive, refresh and minister to your spirit.

This Pocket Encourager can be used in two ways. One, to help you find a relevant scripture and thoughts you need to consider when overtaken by some aspect of discouragement, and two, as a foundation from which you can minister to others whenever they need encouragement.

It goes without saying that the power of this publication lies in the key words of Scripture which it highlights. I have also given some explanations and statements of my own together with a prayer that can be used at the end. In every instance prayer is vital and should be based on Scripture and built around such great themes as God's sovereignty, power, compassion, forgiveness – the same truths that David would undoubtedly have reflected on in those discouraging moments at Ziklag. The thoughts and ideas recorded here have been used in countless counselling situations over the years. Many people have told me they have found them helpful. I hope you will too.

Encouragement must not be regarded as mere sentimentality. We should realise Scripture is equally encouraging when it confronts and challenges us as it is when it consoles and comforts us. To be faced with a challenge when we are hurting may not be what we most want, but it may be what we most need. An African tribe describes medicine that is not too pleasing to the taste but does them good as "It hurts better." Keep in mind that when God challenges us it is only that we might be brought to the place of complete and utter dependency upon Him. God not only lifts the standards to great heights, but also provides the power to reach up to them.

Personally, I find it deeply encouraging that God thinks so much of me that He will not let me get away with things that damage my potential and hinder my effectiveness for Him. *He loves me as I am but He loves me too much to let me stay as I am.* So remember it is still the ministry of encouragement that is at work when Scripture speaks to us in a challenging and confronting way. See these as the Lord's "loving reproofs", for that is just what they are.

May you, like David at Ziklag, learn the skill of encouraging yourself in the Lord your God.

Selwyn Hughes

Selwyn Hughes,
Waverley Abbey House, Farnham, Surrey, England.

POCKET ENCOURAGER

for *Women*

When You Can't Stop
Doing

A few years ago, a heart clinic in America noticed that many of the chairs in their waiting room were getting worn out along the front edge. They started to observe patients in the waiting room and found that many of them sat right on the edge of their chairs, hence the wear and tear on this part of the chairs. This led them to look more deeply into the behaviour of their heart patients.

They found that such people live in the fast lane; drive fast, eat fast, talk fast. Not for them a relaxing holiday on the beach. They go scuba diving or hang gliding or hire a car and visit all things of interest in a 50-mile radius. They feel guilty doing nothing. They are often workaholics and can be very ambitious, not just for themselves, but for their ministry, organisation or church.

There is nothing wrong with using time profitably or working hard, within reason. But there is bound to be wear and tear on the individual who is overdoing it.

The Lord Jesus was the most balanced man who ever lived. He was not under time pressures. Despite all the demands on Him, He had time to spend with His Father, with His disciples, and alone. He preached to large crowds but had time to stop and speak to individuals. Is there a lesson here for you?

"He who kneels the most stands best."
D.L. Moody

Bible Verses to Help You

Be still, and know that I am God.
(Psalm 46:10)

Cast all your anxiety on him because he cares for you.
(1 Peter 5:7)

Suggested further reading

Philippians 4:1–9

Reflect and respond

Are you driven?

Do you need to, "let go and let God"?

Should you be spending more time with the Lord, listening to Him?

When Betrayed by a
Friend

There is a terrible sound in the word "betrayed". To betray someone is to deal treacherously with them. In a hard and cruel world such as this we are not surprised when we are hurt by our enemies, but no one expects to be hurt by a friend. Few things, I imagine, would have hurt our Lord more than to be betrayed by one of His own disciples. How do we cope with betrayal?

First, we must take our pain to God and invite Him to invade our hearts with His soothing balm. All painful situations must be faced, even though they do not have to be dwelt upon. We must let God minister to us in our hurt; He is the only One who can "restore the soul".

Because hurt can quickly escalate into resentment, we must also empty our heart of all bitterness and – with the help of the Lord – forgive. Forgiveness, it must be understood, may not always bring about changes in the other person, (nor guarantee that he or she will want to be restored), but it will ensure release for our own soul.

The cross of our Lord Jesus Christ stands and holds out wide appealing arms to all who have been betrayed. It says: "This is how Jesus dealt with His enemies ... and the friend who betrayed Him." In the light of that great fact can we do anything other than forgive?

"When you forgive you in no way change the past – but you sure do change the future."

Bernard Meltzer

Bible Verses to Help You

He makes me lie down in green pastures, he leads me beside quiet waters, he restores my soul.
(Psalm 23:2)

Therefore, as God's chosen people, holy and dearly loved, clothe yourselves with compassion, kindness, humility, gentleness and patience. Bear with each other and forgive whatever grievances you may have against one another. Forgive as the Lord forgave you.
(Colossians 3:12–13)

Suggested further reading

1 Peter 3:8–12

Reflect and respond

Are you harbouring any pain?

Have you forgiven the person who has wronged you?

Ask Father to give you healing grace.

When You Get the
Blame

We live in a culture of blame. Always the cry is: Whose fault is it? Who was to blame? Who should be punished? Graffiti on a Chicago subway stated, Humpty Dumpty was pushed. Manufacturers and accident insurers in the USA are so afraid of being sued, that they go to extreme lengths to try to protect themselves. The cry is, Someone should pay for this.

Studies have shown that the more a victim blames another person for the accident, the more poorly he copes. Anger and bitterness can go on for years. Being unforgiving, angry, resentful and bitter is wrong in God's eyes, but it can also damage our minds and bodies and delay recovery. We teach to forgive and not to harbour bitterness. "Get rid of all bitterness, rage and anger, brawling and slander, along with every form of malice. Be kind and compassionate to one another, forgiving each other, just as in Christ God forgave you" (Ephesians 4:31,32). It may be difficult, almost impossible to do in our own strength, and often we will need God's help and grace to do it, but do it we must if we do not want to be damaged ourselves.

Even more important, we must forgive so that we may be forgiven. "And when you stand praying, if you hold anything against anyone, forgive him, so that your Father in heaven may forgive you your sins" (Mark 11:25).

Deal with the faults of others as gently as with your own.

Chinese Proverb

Bible Verses to Help You

Resentment kills a fool ...
(Job 5:2)

Be kind and compassionate to one another, forgiving each other, just as in Christ God forgave you.
(Ephesians 4:32)

Suggested further reading

Colossians 3:1–15; 1 Corinthians 13:5

Reflect and respond

Are you harbouring resentment or a grudge?

Is there someone you need to forgive?

Love keeps no record of wrongs – look to put right any wrongs this week.

When You're Afraid of
Death

Christian studies on the subject of death show three underlying concerns: the physical fact of dying, the fear of finality, the fear of judgment. Not all three elements are always present, and one or two elements may be stronger in some than others.

People fear the physical fact of dying because of the possibility of great pain, but the beneficent power of modern drugs makes the chances of this remote. A number of thanatologists (people who conduct research into the stages of dying) say that the struggle some people demonstrate in death is largely unconscious, and is more agonising for those looking on than for the person concerned.

The second fear – the fear of finality – need not concern a Christian. Death does not end all. The resurrection of our Lord proves that the spiritual part of us survives death, and that it was death that died, not He.

The third fear – the fear of judgment – is not as strong as it once was in human minds. This is due in no small measure to the fact that fewer people attend church, and that teaching on the final judgment seems in some churches (not all) to be non-existent. No man or woman who knows Christ need fear judgment. God has consumed our sin and incinerated it at Calvary. Our Lord stands as a great wall between penitent sinners and their sin. We simply must rejoice in that.

Other things may perish but a Christian – never.

> *"When the devil reminds you of your problems, you remind him of his defeat."*
> Gabriel Heymans

Bible Verses to Help You

"Where, O death, is your victory? Where, O death, is your sting?" The sting of death is sin, and the power of sin is the law. But thanks be to God! He gives us the victory through our Lord Jesus Christ.
(1 Corinthians 15:55–57)

… as in Adam all die, so in Christ all will be made alive.
(1 Corinthians 15:22)

Suggested further reading

Psalm 23

Reflect and respond

Allow this scripture to infuse your being:

"I give them eternal life, and they shall never perish; no-one can snatch them out of my hand." (John 10:28)

Put on the helmet of salvation to ward off psychological attacks of the enemy.

When Things Get
Too Much

Have you felt like getting away to a desert island, wanting the pain of the pressure to stop? Sometimes it seems as though there is no way out. A loved one dies. We may be deserted by a wife or husband. A relationship is broken off, or the church is in turmoil. Intractable situations like these can be very stressful but you must beware the quick fix. There may be short term gains, but long term consequences.

If you are in a difficult time, take time to pray and ask God's guidance for your next move. It may be that God wants you to go through the testing time. He may want you to learn something specific, to refine you, to enrich you or simply to teach you to become more dependent on Him. If you immediately take things into your own hands you may miss God's opportunity and plan for you.

God has said, "Fear not, for I have redeemed you; I have summoned you by name; you are mine. When you pass through the waters, I will be with you; and when you pass through the rivers, they will not sweep over you. When you walk through the fire, you will not be burned; the flames will not set you ablaze. For I am the Lord, your God, the Holy One of Israel, your Saviour" (Isaiah 43:1–3). So be encouraged. The darkest time is often just before the dawn.

"He can give only according to His might; therefore He always gives more than we ask for."

Martin Luther

Bible Verses to Help You

Blessed is the man who perseveres under trial, because when he has stood the test, he will receive the crown of life that God has promised to those who love him.
(James 1:12)

The name of the Lord is a strong tower; the righteous run to it and are safe.
(Proverbs 18:10)

Suggested further reading

1 Corinthians 10:1–13

Reflect and respond

Are you tempted to sell the future to purchase the present?

Perhaps God wants you to go through the current pressures – talk to Him about it.

When Trusting is
Hard

Do you worry about tomorrow? Do you inwardly struggle to work out whether there will be enough money for food, clothes or enough preaching inspiration? And what about resources and help needed in the home?

Jesus teaches us in simple terms to trust Him one day at a time, and He will provide on that basis. We may sometimes feel as though we have suddenly run into a crisis, but God is never taken by surprise, He knows our needs better than we know ourselves. God's provision is, PRO (before) VISION (seeing), and it is very reassuring to know that He sees our needs in advance.

In Luke 12, starting at verse 22, Jesus says, "Do not worry about your life, what you will eat; or about your body, what you will wear. Life is more than food, and the body more than clothes . . . consider how the lilies grow. They do not labour or spin. Yet I tell you, not even Solomon in all his splendour was dressed like one of these. If that is how God clothes the grass of the field, which is here today, and tomorrow is thrown into the fire, how much more will he clothe you."

Let us take this opportunity to open up ourselves to new areas of trust, and experience a greater dependency on God. By this we can know a greater measure of His faithfulness and provision for our needs.

God makes a promise; faith believes it, hope anticipates it, patience quietly awaits it.

Bible Verses to Help You

Look at the birds of the air; they do not sow or reap or store away in barns, and yet your heavenly Father feeds them. Are you not much more valuable than they?
(Matthew 6:26)

Suggested further reading

Psalm 95:1–11

Reflect and respond

If you feel fearful, don't be afraid to ask someone to pray with you.

Recite Psalm 23 each day for the next week.

When Your Security Is
Shaken

The stressor that affects more people than any other, and causes most stress, is insecurity or uncertainty. When you feel secure you can relax, and get on with your life. But if you feel insecure, you can become anxious, worried, fearful and stressed about the future. You will probably find it difficult to make decisions.

Many people depend on their position or ministry for security, and if things go awry, security goes and anxiety and stress follow. Recently a large group of male and female civil servants who were in a department threatened with privatisation were compared with another group in a department where no threat existed. There was a marked deterioration in the health of the group under threat compared with the secure group.

You may depend on other things – your pension – then you hear of dishonesty or mismanagement in the pension funds and you begin to wonder, is mine safe?

Perhaps you have been depending on your church congregation for encouragement and support; but people are found to have feet of clay and you feel disillusioned and hurt.

Are you stressed because your security has been taken away, or is being threatened, or may be in the future? God is the answer, as He is to everything. He is the only person who is entirely dependable and has made us to find our security only in Him. If you put your trust in Him, you are guaranteed absolute security.

"I have held many things in my hands, and I have lost them all; but whatever I have placed in God's hands, that I still possess."
Martin Luther

Bible Verses to Help You

My people have committed two sins: They have forsaken me, the spring of living water, and have dug their own cisterns, broken cisterns that cannot hold water.
(Jeremiah 2:13)

Some trust in chariots and some in horses, but we trust in the name of the Lord our God.
(Psalm 20:7)

Suggested further reading

Deuteronomy 33:20–27

Reflect and respond

Do you feel insecure, fearful of the future – what are you depending on for your security?

Are these sources utterly dependable?

Only God is fully dependable. Are you building your life on the Rock?

When Your Marriage is
Shaken 1

Many of England's majestic cathedrals are in need of expensive repair. Often the cause for this is from the vibrations caused by traffic which affects the very foundations. An external force, the vehicle traffic, has created internal problems. Before any remedial work can be carried out an inspection and rectification of the foundations are called for.

So it is with marriage. Often external forces act upon our relationship, causing damage and lasting harm. It is not the pressure upon us that causes the damage, but what we are standing on – rock or sand? Are you standing upon the rock of Jesus? Is your marriage based upon God and His Holy Word? The Hebrew words, *Yasad* and *Musad*, are translated as foundation. They are used where what is to be built upon them is to endure and last for many generations. What you put down as a foundation into your marriage will affect not just you, but also your children and your children's children, and even their children.

Such foundations need to be laid with care,

and carefully chosen to withstand the pressures to be inflicted upon them. Within marriage we equally need to lay a quality foundation with care – that can take any storm that comes at you.

Some of the actions to take in laying these foundations are:

Recognising the need to say sorry and to act unselfishly.

Learning to communicate and express your feelings.

Learn to trust each other and God.

> *"A successful marriage demands a divorce; a divorce from your own self-love."*
>
> Paul Frost

Bible Verses to Help You

Love is patient, love is kind. It does not envy, it does not boast, it is not proud. It is not rude, it is not self-seeking, it is not easily angered, it keeps no record of wrongs. Love does not delight in evil but rejoices with the truth. It always protects, always trusts, always hopes, always perseveres. Love never fails. (1 Corinthians 13:4–8)

The foundations were laid with large stones of good quality. (1 Kings 7:10)

Suggested further reading

Nehemiah 1:1–2

Reflect and respond

Foundations can be beautiful and adorned. They can also reflect the beauty of the finished work.

Read and meditate on Revelation 21:18–21.

When Your Marriage is
Shaken 2

Every marriage can hit problems. At such times it can help to refocus our thoughts if we reflect on what we actually did on our wedding day when we covenanted together in the presence of God (Genesis 2:24).

In the Bible the word covenant is taken from two Hebrew words, *karoth berith,* which means to cut a covenant. In the Old Testament the sacrifice was cut in two, and in the New Testament it was the body of Jesus that was cut by the nails and the spear. In marriage there is the need to cut something, perhaps the ties with home. On a wedding day the symbols of cutting, sacrifice and covenant are there for all to see if we look.

As the bride walks down the aisle she symbolises the sacrifice both families have made in bringing up their children. The groom stands at the front awaiting his bride to symbolise the day Jesus will receive His Bride (Revelation 22:17). The groom stands away from his family to symbolise he has left his father and mother – a cutting away. The bride is given away, again to symbolise a leaving. Rings are exchanged to symbolise a joining together. Cutting of the wedding cake is to symbolise the cutting of a covenant. The toast symbolises that one day those of us who are in Christ will lift up the cup and drink of the new wine with Jesus in heaven (Matthew 26:29).

Whenever a marriage faces problems it is good to reflect on what was actually done on the wedding day.

A deaf husband and a blind wife are always a happy couple.

French Proverb

Bible Verses to Help You

According to the word that I covenanted with you …
Haggai 2:5 (NKJ)

The man said, "This is now bone of my bones and flesh of my flesh; she shall be called 'woman', for she was taken out of man." For this reason a man will leave his father and mother and be united to his wife, and they will become one flesh.
(Genesis 2:23–24)

Suggested further reading

Genesis 17:1–7

Reflect and respond

Are you in a crisis because you have not realised what plans God had for you on your wedding day?

Are you resisting God in your life or marriage?

Ask God, in prayer, what plans He has for both of you.

When the Demands Get
Too Much

Whether you are a mother, wife, hold down a full time job or all three, as a woman your life can sometimes seem to be filled with demands to help others with their spiritual, emotional and physical needs. And because you love them you find yourself in the position of a servant. You are in good company!

Jesus not only taught and encouraged His disciples to serve one another, He lived out His words by His lifestyle, when for example He took a towel, knelt before His disciples and washed their feet. He was a servant through and through, it was epitomised in everything He did, yet He was able to balance servanthood with fulfilling His destiny in God. Jesus was able to display a clear servant heart, caring and ministering to those He met. The motive for His actions was always to do the will of His heavenly Father with a heart of love.

The bedrock of your life is your service to God and everything else can be constructed on this foundation. He knows your circumstances better than you do. Have you ever thought that God knows the stresses we are under and the difficulties that we face? He knows when problems accumulate and others don't pull their weight. He knows the burdens we carry and the desires of our hearts.

So let's focus on God, and acknowledge that He is the one we are serving. Let's be open with Him, not only about our practical needs, but also about our feelings and our weaknesses.

> *"Every Christian needs a half hour of prayer each day, except when he is busy, then he needs an hour."*
>
> *St Frances of Sales*

Bible Verses to Help You

Whatever you did for one of the least of these brothers of mine, you did for me.
(Matthew 25:40)

"My grace is sufficient for you, for my power is made perfect in weakness. ... For when I am weak, then I am strong."
(2 Corinthians 12:8–10)

Suggested further reading

John 13:1–17

Reflect and respond

Jesus said that if you give a cup of cold water in His name then you are serving Him.

From where are you drawing your strength?

Do you need to delegate some of your responsibilities?

When Battling with
Worthlessness

We often view our worth according to what the media, and those around us dictate as acceptable. I am of worth when ... I achieve, I am shown love, I am slim. Sometimes, even when we attain these we still don't feel of worth, and as circumstances change so our view of ourselves changes. Jesus said, "The Spirit gives life; the flesh counts for nothing" (John 6:63). So in other words, even if we attain a feeling of worth through our own achievements, it means nothing, it has no place, and on the day of judgment will be frizzled in the fire. Our worth is in what Christ has done for us. It's like having been given an honorary doctorate and then trying to swot for and sit the exam. You already have all you need! *What counts is what you have already been given.*

Have you begun to catch hold of all that is yours in Christ and who you really are as you have been reading these words? Our opinion of ourselves needs to be checked against the truth of God and His Word about us. In Christ we are worth much, but we have to take what we have been given by Him. You can give someone the most precious gift, but if it is never unwrapped, or unwrapped and then not used, it is worthless. It doesn't matter how little you are, it's how big God is!

Key Bible verses:

> *We ... are being transformed into his likeness with ever-increasing glory.*
> *(2 Corinthians 3:18)*

> *He must become greater; I must become less.*
> *(John 3:30)*

Suggested further reading

Philippians 3:1–10

Reflect and respond

The flesh counts for nothing – pursue the spiritual. Catch hold of all that is yours in Christ.

You are designed for dependence upon God.

When Worried about How Things will *Work Out*

Do you worry about how things will work out? Matthew 6 contains Jesus' words of revelation concerning worry. In the NIV the heading is "Do Not Worry". In the NASB version, the title is, "The Cure for Anxiety". I like that because it offers hope. There is an answer!

When in the midst of despair it can seem as though you work and work at change and yet very little seems to happen. The "working at it" soon becomes a burden. Jesus says, "Come to me, all you who are weary and burdened, and I will give you rest. Take my yoke upon you and learn from me, for I am gentle and humble in heart, and you will find rest for your souls. For my yoke is easy and my burden is light" (Matthew 11:28–30). Jesus' burden is light and in Him there is rest for the weary. Doesn't it feel exhausting carrying your load?

Allowing Jesus to take the load involves "letting go". It means no longer trying to do things our way, but allowing the Holy Spirit to have control. In Galatians Paul speaks about the flesh and about the Spirit. He describes the manifestations of the flesh as works and the manifestations of the Spirit as fruit. The first requires effort, the second involves surrender. It you are tired of working at your problems, surrender them to God.

"A life in thankfulness releases the glory of God."

Bengt Sundberg

Bible Verses to Help You

"Cast all your anxiety on him because he cares for you."
(1 Peter 5:7)

Do not be anxious about anything, but in everything, by prayer and petition, with thanksgiving, present your requests to God. And the peace of God, which transcends all understanding, will guard your hearts and your minds in Christ Jesus.
(Philippians 4: 6–7)

Suggested further reading

Matthew 6:25–34

Reflect and respond

There is a cure for anxiety – Allowing Jesus to take the load involves "letting go".

Surrender your problem to God today.

When Feeling
Powerless

Yes it's true, we are powerless in our own right! But God does not say, "My power is made perfect in your strength", but "your weakness". Only as we are weak do we see God's strength worked out in our lives. Apparently the eagle is the only bird which renews its wings. As it gets older its wings begin to make a noise and its beak grows calluses, which means that it is less able to catch its prey. So it takes itself off somewhere safe and plucks out all its feathers and rubs the growth off its beak. New feathers grow. We need to go through a similar process: to shed our feathers, let go of what we have relied on to survive and let God give us His feathers.

Maybe you don't know the authority and power that is rightfully yours through Christ. If Jesus is the head over all power and authority and He lives in you, this gives you power and authority. *In order to exercise authority, a person has to submit to a higher authority.* As you submit to Jesus in each area of your life, so you can command anything which is not of Him to go. The secret is not to say, "I believe it will change", but to command in the name of Jesus for it to change, and then live in the truth that it has changed.

"I'm a thousand times bigger on the inside than I am on the outside."

Smith Wigglesworth

Bible Verses to Help You

"My grace is sufficient for you, for my power is made perfect in weakness."
(2 Corinthians 12:9)

The Lord will fight for you; you need only to be still."
(Exodus 14:14)

Suggested further reading

Ephesians 1:3–10

Reflect and respond

God's power is made perfect in our weakness.

Those who put their hope in the Lord will renew their strength.

You have all power and authority through Christ – begin to pray into your situation with that authority!

14

When Devotion Seems
Costly

The story of the woman with an alabaster jar of very expensive perfume is quite beautiful. She broke the jar and poured the perfume on the head of Jesus, and yet some of those present rebuked her harshly.

"'Leave her alone,' said Jesus. 'Why are you bothering her? She has done a beautiful thing to me. The poor you will always have with you, and you can help them any time you want. But you will not always have me. She did what she could. … I tell you the truth, wherever the gospel is preached throughout the world, what she has done will also be told, in memory of her'" (Mark 14:6–9).

I find this an amazing story, how a woman who was a social outcast and a nobody, could publicly waste probably everything she had on someone she loved. Maybe she was impetuous and impulsive, I don't know, but she took what she had and used the opportunity that came her way to anoint Jesus. As far as we know this was the only time that Jesus was ever anointed. For her this was an ultimate expression of demonstrating her love with everything she had. In the words of Jesus "she has done a beautiful thing." What a wonderful way to express love! It didn't seem to matter to her that she was criticised for being extravagant or uneconomical, for sacrificial love is never economical.

There may be times when other people shake their heads at the extravagance of one life devoted to another, but this is a real expression of what love is all about.

> *"God is love, He doesn't merely have it or give it; He gives Himself."*
>
> *Joseph Fletcher*

Bible Verses to Help You

"She has done a beautiful thing to me."
(Mark 14:6)

"... she loved much. But he who has been forgiven little loves little."
(Luke 7:47)

Suggested further reading

1 Corinthians 13:4–8

Reflect and respond

Jesus said that the reason the woman loved much was because she knew she'd been forgiven much.

The more we realise how much God loves us, the more we will be able to pour out His love for others.

15

When I Can't Understand Why God Allows Events in My *Life*

Since God formed you in your mother's womb He has been continually at work in your life, moulding and shaping you, as He transforms you into His likeness. God's purpose for your life is that you should become like Him.

Have you ever seen a potter at work as he takes a lump of raw clay, and with all his dexterity and expertise, he forms it into something beautiful and unique. The prophet Isaiah says, "O Lord, you are our Father. We are the clay, you are the potter; we are all the work of your hand" (Isaiah 64:8). God is committed to working in every department of our lives where He has access.

The Bible also likens God's dealings with us to that of a gold or silver refiner. This craft required a lot of care as the refiner sat beside a pan of molten metal and skimmed off the dross which rose to the surface. This process took much time and attention, and would only be complete when the refiner could see his face reflected in the precious metal.

It would be easy for us to think that growth in

our lives happens through the good things with which we are blessed, and the high spots which leave us with lasting memories. This may be true, but it is even more true to say that God uses the difficult times and hardships to strengthen our character and bring us further on our journey along the road to maturity.

Take heart, knowing that whatever we face in our daily lives, God can use as an opportunity for us to prove Him in new ways.

> *"God's purpose is bigger than your problem."*
>
> Larry Lea

Bible Verses to Help You

Yet, O Lord, you are our Father. We are the clay, you are the potter; we are all the work of your hand.
(Isaiah 64:8)

And we know that in all things God works for the good of those who love him, who have been called according to his purpose.
(Romans 8:28)

Suggested further reading

Psalm 37:1–11

Reflect and respond

Your life in God is a living process towards maturity. If you submit, He will support.

Prayer: "Help me Lord to see any difficult circumstances as your opportunities."

16

When One Thing Comes After
Another

"When sorrows come, they come not single spies, but in battalions," said Shakespeare in *Hamlet*. We all know how true this is! Troubles have an uncanny way of coming together. For a while everything goes along pleasantly and then suddenly the whole world tumbles around our ears. Nobody fully understands why it is that troubles seem to arrive in swarms. Many have tried to explain this strange rhythmic law, but when all has been said it still remains a mystery.

What is not a mystery, though, is that God never withdraws from us no matter how many troubles we face. We must learn that in times of difficulty and stress, we come to a fresh and vivid realisation of our dependency on God. When things are going well we have confidence in our ability to look after our own affairs. We feel we are able to handle things alone. But when diffi-culties crowd in upon us and hedge us in on every side then our confidence evaporates, we are reminded in a dramatic way of our frailty and cry out to the Lord for His help. We realise we are not as strong and as self-sufficient as we thought we were.

That discovery is worth making. It produces in us a humility that compels us to lift up praying hands to the Lord. We learn best the meaning of dependency on God not on the starlit way but on the shadowed way.

I am an old man and have known a great many troubles, but most of them never happened.

Mark Twain

Bible Verses to Help You

Have mercy on me, O God, have mercy on me, for in you my soul takes refuge. I will take refuge in the shadow of your wings until the disaster has passed.
(Psalm 57:1)

Then they cried out to the Lord in their trouble, and he brought them out of their distress. He stilled the storm to a whisper; the waves of the sea were hushed.
(Psalm 107:28–29)

Suggested further reading

James 1:1–4

Reflect and respond

Acknowledge before God that you are totally dependent on Him.

Seek assurance from the Scriptures that God will never leave you.

Rejoice that you can trust God perfectly.

17

When Plagued by Feelings of
Inferiority

Frequently in these modern times one hears the term "inferiority complex" bandied about. It is often used to describe the low sense of worth many women carry around with them, usually the consequence of ineffective parenting. A low sense of worth may blight a whole life and at its worst can develop into self-rejection, even hate. Most women learn how to cope with the problem by keeping away from situations in which they might be shown up as inferior, and thus live their lives at a lower level than God intends.

Whatever forces have gone into shaping our thoughts and ideas about ourselves (and we must be careful not to hold bitterness or resentment against those who nurtured us), we who are Christians must stand before God and draw the estimate of ourselves from Him. However little worth there may be in our nature, God put worth upon us by dying for our salvation. No one is to be despised (not even by him or herself) when they were dear enough to God that He shed

His sacred blood. That is the ground of our worth, the solid, sufficient and only basis for it. And it is the same for everyone.

This last statement must be allowed to soak into our minds, for it is only when we see that worth is not something that is earned but something bestowed that self-despising can be rooted out of our minds.

What other people think of me is becoming less and less important; what they think of Jesus because of me is critical.

Cliff Richard

Bible Verses to Help You

Therefore, there is now no condemnation for those who are in Christ Jesus ...
(Romans 8:1)

So you are no longer a slave, but a son; and since you are a son, God has made you also an heir.
(Galatians 4:7)

Suggested further reading

Ephesians 2:1–7

Reflect and respond

Do you recognise something in your history that contributed to your low esteem?

Have you asked a close friend or minister to pray through some of the issues with you?

Ask God to infuse you with the revelation of your status in Christ.

18

When There's Problems in the
Home

"Life," as Hemingway put it, "breaks us all," but few things are as painful as being broken by difficult circumstances in the home. What kind of troubles bring us to breaking point in the home? An unfaithful or unloving partner, disobedient or rebellious children, constant bickering and rows, misunderstandings, financial pressures, living with difficult in-laws, infirmity or sickness ... and so on. Many, out of loyalty to their families, face the world with a smile, but inwardly they are torn and bleeding.

A study made at Rhode Island University concluded that one of the most dangerous places on this planet was the average American home. To survive the problems that can arise in the home we must first be secure in our identity as a person, only then can we be secure as a partner or a parent. If we draw our life and energy from those around us, rather than from God then when difficulties arise we will soon find ourselves spiritually bankrupt. No husband, father, mother, son or daughter is able to meet the deep needs of our soul, quite simply, they are not enough. God is the only One able to do that. It is from Him and Him alone that we are able to draw the energy and strength to relate well to others, and when we attempt to draw that energy from others and not Him we quickly run out of coping ability.

Unless the Lord builds the house, its builders labour in vain.

Psalm 127:1

Bible Verses to Help You

"And my God will meet all your needs according to his glorious riches in Christ Jesus."
(Philippians 4:19)

Love is patient, love is kind.
(1 Corinthians 13:4)

Suggested further reading

Hebrews 12:10–15

Reflect and respond

Are there any practical things you can do to change the atmosphere of your home?

Ask God to give you the strength to effect things by what you do rather than what you say.

Spend time with the Father – draw the energy you need from Him.

19

When Marriage Roles get
Confused

Behind every great man is a great woman! The wife's role is to respect her husband. Or, to put it another way the wife is to support her husband. Is your role like that, or are you kicking against it because of outside pressure and afraid of being seen as going against the flow?

Perhaps it is in the nature of humanity, for some of us to be more submissive than others, "responders" rather than "initiators". But we are still individual people – able to speak for ourselves. We have special talents, our own ideas, interests, likes and dislikes and, of course, we are equal heirs in the grace of God (1 Peter 3:7).

A happy marriage is usually one which is balanced. Uneven marriages don't work. If they are all submission or all authority, the scales are weighted against them. Wives are a balance to their husbands, to complement them, recognising their authority in God. The dictionary definition of complement is "completeness" or "perfection", which is something for us to aim at in our marriage.

According to Matthew Henry's commentary, "Woman was not made out of his head to rule over him, nor out of his feet to be trampled upon by him, but out of his side to be equal with him, under his arm to be protected, and near his heart to be loved."

A good husband makes a good wife.

Woman was the final creative act of God, with her He finished and said it "was very good" (Genesis 1:31).

Marriage is a partnership between equals, with different roles to play. But each role needs the other. Perhaps a bit like an aeroplane – the wings keep it up and the tail keeps it in a straight line. Lose one and something serious happens.

Bible Verses to Help You

"... the wife must respect her husband."
(Ephesians 5:33)

... and the two will become one flesh.
(Matthew 19:5)

Suggested further reading

Ephesians 5:21–33

Reflect and respond

Ask God to strengthen your desire to fulfil your role as a wife.

Talk and pray with your husband about your different roles in marriage and how these should work out practically.

20

When God Seems
Far Away

Sometimes even mature Christians who have followed the Lord for many years go through times when God seems very far away. In the main there are three possible reasons for this.

First, the problem can stem from a purely physical cause. Sickness, stress or overwork can affect our moods to such a degree that we think we are spiritually low when the real problem lies in a poor physical condition. This is why God gave Elijah a period of rest and recuperation (see 1 Kings 19).

Second, God might seem far away because of sin. God has so built our spiritual system that when we sin, conviction descends. In this situation repentance is the only way back. Repentance, remember, means more than just "being sorry" it means being sorry enough to quit. When repentance has taken effect we can be sure that our relationship with God will be restored.

The third reason – and by far the most common one – for feeling that God is far away is because we fail to take the time to maintain our relationship with Him. If we don't take the time to talk to God regularly in prayer and listen to Him through reading His Word, then ought it to surprise us that the relationship between us and Him begins to deteriorate? As someone put it: "if God seems far away – guess who moved?" God never moves away from us – it's we who move away from Him.

> *"Thou hast made us for Thyself, O Lord; and our heart is restless until it rests in Thee."*
>
> *St Augustine*

Bible Verses to Help You

God has said, "Never will I leave you; never will I forsake you." (Hebrews 13:5b)

"God did this so that men would seek him and perhaps reach out for him and find him, though he is not far from each one of us. 'For in him we live and move and have our being.'" (Acts 17:27–28)

Suggested further reading

Psalm 139:7–10

Reflect and respond

Do you need a physical health check-up?

Have you dealt with any unresolved sin?

Have you spent quality time with God lately?

21

When Fear
Transcends

Fear, it must be said at once, can be a friend as well as a foe. A healthy fear keeps us from rushing across a traffic-infested street, it compels caution and preserves life. An unhealthy fear however, can quickly enslave the whole personality.

How does Christ enable His children to deal with fear? He does it by imparting to us the energy and power to face anything that comes, assuring us that whatever the difficulties we have to face, we can be more than a match for them, in Him. The apostle Paul puts it like this.. "For God did not give us a spirit of timidity, but a spirit of power, of love and of self-discipline" (2 Timothy 1:7).

The one thing that underlies all unhealthy fear is the desire for avoidance. The fearful heart says: "When afraid – avoid." The Holy Spirit however, enables us to face whatever it is that troubles us, knowing that no matter what happens it can never separate us from God and His unending love. The apostle John says, "Perfect love drives out fear" (1 John 4:18). Resting in His love – a love that will never let us go – we can move into any situation that makes us afraid with a confidence that transcends all fear. Fear says, "Avoid". Faith says, "Confront". Therefore move with God towards the thing you fear and just see what God will do.

Bible Verses to Help You

Even though I walk through the valley of the shadow of death, I will fear no evil, for you are with me; your rod and your staff, they comfort me.
(Psalm 23:4)

The Lord is my light and my salvation – whom shall I fear?
(Psalm 27:1)

Suggested further reading

Psalm 46:1–2

Reflect and respond

Is your fear a godly or worldly fear?

Have you strengthened your spirit with the Word?

Have you been avoiding rather than confronting your fear?

22

When Facing
Loneliness

Loneliness often arises from circumstances beyond our control (when we are shut in by sickness or disability, for example). But loneliness can also come from an inability to relate well to others. When we are lonely because of life's circumstances we must never forget that nothing can interfere with our communion with heaven. Shut off from others we can still have contact with the Friend of friends – Jesus

Many people, though, are lonely not by reason of their circumstances but because of an inability to relate. In a needy world like ours, it has been said, anyone can have friendship who will give friendship. A very lonely individual became someone who was sought after by many after he heard his pastor say in a sermon, "The best way to have a friend is to be a friend." He went home, got down on his knees and prayed, "Lord, forgive me for focusing more on myself than others. From now on I will move towards others with the same love by which You move towards me." As his thoughts changed from self-centredness to other-centredness he became a more interesting and attractive personality. His circle of friends widened and he became outgoing in all his relationships.

The best way to have a friend is to be a friend.

No Christian is ever without the friendship of God, but when lacking the friendship of human beings, keep in mind that when we give ourselves to others they will often give themselves to us.

Bible Verses to Help You

Then you will call, and the Lord will answer; you will cry for help, and he will say: Here am I.
(Isaiah 58:9)

Come near to God and he will come near to you.
(James 4:8)

Suggested further reading

Psalm 139:1–18

Reflect and respond

Have you drawn close to your Heavenly friend – Jesus?

Have you made yourself a friend to others?

Could you do more to focus on others rather than yourself?

23

When Forgiving is Not *Easy*

Some think Christianity sets an impossible standard when it calls on believers to forgive all those who have hurt or injured them. But with God "all things are possible". There are three main reasons why we may find it difficult to forgive. First, we do not have a sufficiently deep realisation of how much we ourselves have been forgiven. The sin of another against us is as nothing when compared to our sin against God – yet He has forgiven us.

Second, holding resentment or indignation against another who has hurt us gives us a sense of power and control over them, and when we give it up, we are left feeling somewhat helpless. But it is to helplessness we are called in the words: "'It is mine to avenge, I will repay,' says the Lord" (Romans 12:19). Forgiveness involves giving up control and trusting God with the outcome.

A third reason is what we might call "misplaced dependency". This occurs when we move from dependency on God to dependency on others.

Then when they hurt us, we stumble because we believe we need them in order to function. This is why we are always hurt most by those who are c losest to us.

Forgiveness, we must remember, is not so much a feeling but a decision – an action of the will. You decide to forgive, whether you feel like it or not. *You supply the willingness, God will supply the power.*

"The greatest single cause of atheism in the world today is Christians who acknowledge Jesus with their lips, then walk out the door and deny Him by their lifestyle. ..."
Brennan Manning

Bible Verses to Help You

Bear with each other and forgive whatever grievances you may have against one another. Forgive as the Lord forgave you.
(Colossians 3:13)

... as far as the east is from the west, so far has he removed our transgressions from us.
(Psalm 103:12)

Suggested further reading

2 Corinthians 2:8–11

Reflect and respond

Do you feel overwhelmed with your unforgiveness? Go to the Father with your problem.

Have you made the decision to forgive?

24

When You No Longer Want to
Pray

The obstacles to prayer are many. Some claim they don't have time to pray, others that they have no place to pray. Well, it's always possible to go for a walk with Jesus. Still others complain they don't know what to pray for. Then make a list – friends and loved ones who need to be converted, those known to you who are sick, the needs of the church you attend, your own needs, and so on.

By far the most common obstacle to prayer, however, is disinclination. People do not pray because they do not feel like it. But we must not assume that prayer is effective only when it arises from an eager and emotional heart. Those who have achieved great power in prayer tell us that floods of feeling come only now and again in their times of intercession. It we have an appointment to meet someone whom we regard as important, do we break it a few moments before the meeting because we feel disinclined? Common courtesy tells us it would not be right. Are we to be less courteous with God?

The great practitioners of prayer assure us God can do more with us when we pray against our inclination than when we pray with it. The willingness to submit to Him deepens our surrender; our resolve to go to God builds steel into our Christian commitment. It is faith, not feeling, that measures the efficacy of prayer.

> "Intercessory prayer might be defined as loving our neighbour on our knees."
>
> *Charles Brent*

Bible Verses to Help You

And pray in the Spirit on all occasions with all kinds of prayers and requests. With this in mind, be alert and always keep on praying for all the saints.
(Ephesians 6:18)

I cry aloud to the Lord; I lift up my voice to the Lord for mercy. I pour out my complaint before him; before him I tell my trouble.
(Psalm 142:1–6)

Suggested further reading

Psalm 42:5–11

Reflect and respond

Are you always making excuses not to pray?

Have you persevered above your feelings?

Submit your prayers to God in faith – just do it!

25

When Doubts
Crowd In

Many Christians feel that if doubt exists in their minds they cannot be true believers. This arises from a wrong understanding of the nature of doubt. "Doubt," says Os Guinness, "is a state of mind in suspension between faith and unbelief so that it is neither of them wholly, and it is each only partly. It is faith in two minds."

Perhaps we can better understand doubt by taking the analogy of fear. Many think fear is the opposite of courage, but it is not. The opposite of fear is cowardice. Fear is the half-way stage between the two. It is not wrong to feel fear in certain situations. The real question is what do we do with it–something courageous or something cowardly? It is the same with doubt. It stands undecided between faith and unbelief and has to choose between the two.

A man one day came to Jesus and confessed to his struggle with doubt (Mark 9:14–29). The struggle with doubt must be seen as a sign of faith, not unbelief.

What destroys faith is not doubt but disobedience – the unwillingness to bring those doubts and lay them at the feet of Jesus. The prayer of the man in the incident referred to, "I do believe; help me overcome my unbelief!" is one that all of us must echo whenever we are caught in the throes of doubt. This attitude changes everything.

> "Believe your beliefs and doubt your doubts."
>
> *F. F. Bosworth*

Bible Verses to Help You

Then he said to Thomas, "Put your finger here; see my hands. Reach out your hand and put it into my side. Stop doubting and believe." Thomas said to him, "My Lord and my God!" (John 20:27–28)

Immediately Jesus reached out his hand and caught him. "You of little faith," he said, "why did you doubt?" (Matthew 14:31)

Suggested further reading

Job 42:1–5

Reflect and respond

Stop mentally beating yourself up when you doubt.

Do you wallow in doubt, or use it as a springboard to faith?

Call upon God to deliver you from doubt.

26

When Dealing with
Failure

It's hard to look objectively at things when one has failed. When Millais first exhibited his "Ophelia" in 1852 one critic dubbed it "O Failure!" It is said that Millais was plagued by these words for the rest of his life.

When overtaken by failure sit down as soon as possible and prayerfully begin to analyse the reason for the failure. Consider the possibility that God may have allowed this failure because it was part of His purpose for your life. Many have discovered that God allowed failure in their life to turn their thoughts in a new direction of service for Him.

If, however, after prayer and careful consideration of this possibility you are sure you have God's approval for continuing along the same lines, then ask yourself, Have I contributed to this failure by wrong timing, failure to weigh up the pros and cons, disregard of moral principles, insensitivity to other people's feelings ... and so on? Having learned the lessons that come from failure – try again.

A Christian poster I once saw showed a man in a T-shirt with the admission "I gave up". In the corner of the poster, barely visible, was a drawing of a little black hill and on it a very tiny cross. These words were printed beneath it: "I didn't". The One who triumphed over all obstacles holds out His hands to you. Take His hand and if another purpose has not been shown you – try again.

> *"The worst is not to fail, but to give up."*
> Ed Cole

Bible Verses to Help You

If the Lord delights in a man's way, he makes his steps firm; though he stumble, he will not fall, for the Lord upholds him with his hand.
(Psalm 37:23–24)

I press on towards the goal to win the prize for which God has called me heavenwards in Christ Jesus.
(Philippians 3:14)

Suggested further reading

Proverbs 3:1–5

Reflect and respond

Are your goals God's goals?

Have you taken responsibility for your own actions?

Trust God to deliver you from your circumstances

27

When Hopes are *Dashed*

Hope is one of the cardinal values of the Christian faith. "... these three remain," said the apostle Paul in 1 Corinthians 13:13, "faith, hope and love". All through the New Testament, hope is spoken of in the highest terms.

We must differentiate, however, between the word "hope" as it is used in Scripture and the way it is used in ordinary conversation. Sometimes people say, "I hope things will get better", or "I am hoping for an increase in my salary", but we are not given any guarantees in Scripture that everything we "hope" for in this sense will come our way. When the Bible talks about "hope" it is talking about the certainty we have as Christians that God's eternal purposes will never be thwarted. The thing that gives a Christian what the writer to the Hebrews calls a hope "both sure and steadfast" (Hebrews 6:19, AV) is the fact that God is on the throne. Have you noticed in the Scriptures that whenever God's servants were in trouble they were given a vision of the eternal throne? Isaiah ... David ...

Ezekiel ... the apostle John. Why a throne? Because God rules from His throne, and no matter if appearances are to the contrary, He is always in control. The hope (or certainty) that God's purposes continue even if ours get pushed aside acts as an anchor to the soul. We must never forget it.

"Fulfilment of your destiny does not come in a moment, a month, or a year, but over a lifetime."

Casey Treat

Bible Verses to Help You

We have this hope as an anchor for the soul, firm and secure. It enters the inner sanctuary behind the curtain ...
(Hebrews 6:19)

Know therefore that the Lord your God is God; he is the faithful God, keeping his covenant of love to a thousand generations of those who love him and keep his commands.
(Deuteronomy 7:9)

Suggested further reading

Hebrews 11

Reflect and respond

Is your hope in God or in mere speculation?

Have you allowed His Word to fuel your hope?

Trust the Father, and watch your hope soar.

28

When You Fall into Grievous
Sin

Sin, it has been said, is not so much the break-ing of God's laws as the breaking of His heart. How then do we relieve the hurt that lies upon the heart of God when we have fallen into griev-ous sin?

First, we must not minimise the sin. Nowadays there is a tendency to describe a moral mishap as just a "little" thing, or "it wasn't important". Cancer in the stomach is still cancer even though a person may pass off their discomfort as "a bit of indigestion". We don't make a deadly thing innocuous by giving it a different name.

Second, we must confess the sin to God. We must cry out to Him as did the psalmist, "Have mercy on me, O God, according to your unfailing love ... blot out my transgressions. Wash away all my iniquity and cleanse me from my sin" (Psalm 51:1–2).

Third, if the sin has involved others then we must seek to put things right with them also. It is always helpful to discuss this matter with a minister or a Christian counsellor, however, before embarking on a course of action so as to avoid unnecessary complications.

Fourth, we must walk into the future clean and more dependent than ever on God's empowering grace. All the resources of heaven are engaged against sin, and the reason why we fall into it is because we do not avail ourselves of those resources.

"Get alone with Jesus – and either tell Him that you do not want sin to die out in you – or else tell Him that at all costs you want to be identified with His death."

Oswald Chambers

Bible Verses to Help You

If we confess our sins, he is faithful and just and will forgive us our sins and purify us from all unrighteousness.
(1 John 1:9)

Blessed is he whose transgressions are forgiven, whose sins are covered. Blessed is the man whose sin the Lord does not count against him and in whose spirit is no deceit.
(Psalm 32:1–2)

Suggested further reading

James 4:6–10

Reflect and respond

Have you taken responsibility for your sin?

Have you confessed your sin and settled things with others?

Look to your future with a clean heart and lean upon His grace.

29

When the Stress Becomes
Too Much

Experts on stress tell us it comes from two main causes: too little change and too much change. Dr Thomas Holmes, a recognised authority on stress, measures it in terms of "units of change". The death of a loved one, for example, measures 100 units, a divorce 73 units, pregnancy 40 units, moving or refurbishing a home 25 units, and Christmas is given 12 units. His conclusion is that no one can handle more than 300 units of stress in a 12-month period without suffering physically or emotionally during the next two years.

The first thing to do when experiencing stress is to identify what is causing it. What is the trigger? What are the symptoms? What happened immediately prior to the symptoms occurring? (This can be a vital clue.) We must invite the Lord to help with the matter as we think and pray it through. Only when the cause is found can things be changed.

Next, we must consider why it is that we are victims of stress. Are we unable to move ahead because of fear, or are we going too fast because we are afraid of what we might discover about ourselves if we stopped? To the degree we lack security in God, to that degree we will be motivated to find it in something else. *The secure are less prone to stress because they already have what they want – inner peace of mind.*

"Oh, how great peace and quietness would he possess who should cut off all vain anxiety and place all his confidence in God."

Thomas à Kempis

Bible Verses to Help You

Take my yoke upon you and learn from me, for I am gentle and humble in heart, and you will find rest for your souls.
(Matthew 11:29)

Peace I leave with you; my peace I give you. I do not give to you as the world gives. Do not let your hearts be troubled and do not be afraid.
(John 14:27)

Suggested further reading

Psalm 139:1–7

Reflect and respond:

Have you identified what is causing your stress?

Have you included God in the process of deliverance from stress?

Put your security in God today.

30

When Coping with
Depression

Almost everyone, from time to time, will confess to feelings of depression, but usually
these feelings quickly pass. When they continue
for a few weeks, however, and become increas-
ingly acute, then medical opinion should be
sought, if only to ascertain whether or not the
cause is physical.

Many things can plunge us into a low mood –
uncertainty about the future, a breakdown in
relationships, financial difficulties, ageing, lack of
purpose, and so on. The common denominator,
though, with deeply depressed feelings is a sense
of loss. A vital clue also to understanding what
plunges us into depression is found when we
examine the relationship between what we are
doing and the expected rewards. If our actions
and behaviours do not, over a period of time,
bring us the rewards we expect then we can
become so discouraged that we sink into a
low mood.

The best remedy for all non-biological depression is to gain a new perspective – to turn one's

gaze from earth to heaven. The psalmist in Psalm 42 sees that there is a thirst inside him that no one can meet except God. When he looks to God for the satisfaction of that thirst (rather than others), his soul then rests on the hope that no matter what happens, he remains secure as a person. Understanding this, and constantly applying it in our lives, is the key to overcoming and remaining free from depression.

Even though I walk through the valley of the shadow of death, I will fear no evil, for you are with me; your rod and your staff, they comfort me.

Psalm 23

Bible Verses to Help You

Why are you downcast, O my soul? Why so disturbed within me? Put your hope in God, for I will yet praise him, my Saviour and my God.
(Psalm 42:5)

The Lord is close to the broken-hearted and saves those who are crushed in spirit.
(Psalm 34:18)

Suggested further reading

Psalm 32:1–7

Reflect and respond

Is your depression medically related?

Is your gaze towards heaven or earth?

Thirst after God and regain your hope.

31

When You Doubt that God is
Good

"The root of sin," said Oswald Chambers, "is the belief that God is not good." There are a multitude of circumstances and events we have to face in a fallen world that suggest God is not good – earthquakes, famines, storms and floods that wipe out whole communities, disease, and so on.

Before radar was invented, the art of navigation depended on the existence of fixed points. Mariners took their bearings not from a cloud or a floating spar but from the stars and from things that were solid, such as a headland or a lighthouse. If a seaman took a bearing and found he was off course he would not doubt the star or the headland – he would doubt himself.

We need to do the same whenever we find ourselves doubting that God is good. We must see to it that we are fixed to the things that are fixed. The cross is one of those things. It is the irrefutable proof that God is love. When we look around and consider the many situations that seem to give the lie to the fact that God is love, we must not pretend these matters do not cause us problems. Rather, we must set them all over against the one thing that is crystal clear – God's love as demonstrated for us on Calvary. A God who would do that for us simply must be Love. *At the foot of Calvary the ground is fixed.*

"In the maddening maze of things,
And tossed by storm and flood,
To one fixed trust my spirit clings:
I know that God is good!"

John Greenleaf Whittier

Bible Verses to Help You

"Why do you call me good?" Jesus answered. "No-one is good – except God alone."
(Mark 10:18)

For God so loved the world that he gave his one and only Son, that whoever believes in him shall not perish but have eternal life. For God did not send his Son into the world to condemn the world, but to save the world through him.
(John 3:16–17)

Suggested further reading

1 Peter 2:1–5

Reflect and respond

Is your thinking grounded in the Scriptures?

Have you confused worldly circumstances with God's will?

Fix your eyes once again on Calvary and God's love displayed there.

32

When Facing Bitter
Disappointment

Hardly any of us can go through life without experiencing on occasions the dampening effect of disappointment. A friend we hoped would come through for us lets us down, an event on which we pinned a great deal of hope fails to materialise, an important promise made to us is broken. Dealing with such disappointments is not easy. The following three principles, however, when followed and practised should help.

First, we must accept that what has happened has happened. When, in the effort to get away from the pain of disappointment, we pretend that something has not happened, or that it has happened in a different way, we deceive ourselves. Integrity requires that whatever is true, whatever is real, must be faced.

Second, we must acknowledge our feelings – if we feel hurt, angry, frustrated, or any other negative emotions, we must be willing to face them. Unacknowledged emotions invariably cause trouble.

Third, we must bring the issue to God in prayer, remembering that He can take every one of life's disappointments and make them work for us rather than against us (see Romans 8:28–29). Just change the first letter of "Disappointment" from "D" to "H" and "*Disappointment*" becomes "*His-appointment*".

Bible Verses to Help You

And we know that in all things God works for the good of those who love him, who have been called according to his purpose.
(Romans 8:28)

Trust in the Lord with all your heart and lean not on your own understanding; in all your ways acknowledge him, and he will make your paths straight.
(Proverbs 3:5–6)

Suggested further reading

Proverbs 16:1–9

Reflect and respond

Accept what has happened, or not happened, and bring your feelings to God knowing that He never disappoints.

33

When You Need Divine
Guidance

Few Christians have difficulty believing in the personal guidance of God. For the most part our difficulty is not with the fact that God guides but how. Usually God guides along five main routes: through prayerful reading of the Scriptures, through the preaching of God's Word, through reason, through circumstances, and through a strong inner witness. How do these all come together when we are in need of personal guidance?

Some people have found God's guidance while prayerfully reading His Word, as a certain verse is quickened to them. Others have heard His voice through a sermon in church. Still others find the divine will by reasoning an issue through, either by themselves or with a godly friend or counsellor. Circumstances can point the way to God's will also. Things may get chaotic, but often God shakes our circumstances to move us in a different direction.

Then finally there is what some Christians call the way of peace. To find guidance it can help to look at the various options open to you, then picture yourself going down them one by one. On one of these paths a deeper peace may rest. Not a thrill, not pleasure, but peace. This may be the road down which God wants you to travel. Remember, however, it's always good to share all your conclusions about God's guidance, if you can, with a wise and godly friend.

"Abraham did not know the way, but he knew the Guide."

Lee Robertson

Bible Verses to Help You

I will instruct you and teach you in the way you should go; I will counsel you and watch over you.
(Psalm 32:8)

Your word is a lamp to my feet and a light for my path.
(Psalm 119:105)

Suggested further reading

Psalm 25:1–5

Reflect and respond

What have you done so far to seek God for guidance?

Have you sought Him in His Word and with prayer?

Have you established an "inner witness" that brings peace to your circumstances?

34

When You Feel Forgotten by
God

It is forgivable, when overtaken by all kinds of difficulties and problems, to think that we are forgotten by God. Forgivable, but not true. From observation and experience it appears that the Christians who fall prey to this misapprehension are those who struggle with a deep sense of inferiority and see themselves as being of little consequence on this earth. Feeling of little importance on earth they deduce, erroneously, they are of little importance in heaven. The psalmist reminds us in Psalm 139 that God's thoughts are always towards us – and that they are more in number than the grains of sand (v. 18).

But perhaps the greatest verse we can focus our attention on when tempted to think that God has forgotten us is Isaiah 49:16: "See, I have engraved you on the palms of my hands." The palm of the hand has passed into our proverbs as a symbol of familiarity. We sometimes hear people say: "I know it like the palm of my hand." It is on the palm of His hand, says the prophet Isaiah, that God has put our names. And they are not just written there, but engraved there. This means our names are before Him in such a way that they cannot be overlooked. He does not depend on a ministering spirit to bring our names to His attention. They are imprinted there – on the palms of His hands.

"God's investment in us is so great He could not possibly abandon us."

Erwin W. Lutzer.

Bible Verse to Help You

Can a mother forget the baby at her breast and have no compassion on the child she has borne? Though she may forget, I will not forget you!
(Isaiah 49:15)

Suggested further reading

Exodus 34:1–8

Reflect and respond

Have you swallowed the lie of the enemy that God does not care?

Have you sought the security of the Scriptures to see the true Father?

Bask in the knowledge that God knows you personally.`

35

When Battling with Sexual
Frustration

The hunger for sex, we must recognise, is no more shameful than the hunger for food. However, this should not be taken to mean that, like the hunger for food, it must be indulged. We can't live without food, but we can live without sex.

The main problem underlying sexual frustration is that of the release of sexual energy. With married people this can be done legitimately through the act of sexual intercourse, but for single people this is forbidden by Scripture. How do single people, and in some circumstances married people also, handle a clamant sex drive? Is masturbation the answer? Scripture is relatively silent on this issue, and some feel that when no other relief can be found, masturbation is permissible, providing no sexual images are being entertained.

There is "a more excellent way", though – the way of sublimation. Sublimation is the rechannelling of energies into another and higher level of activity. One of the best practitioners of this was the apostle Paul. He was creative at the place of the mind and spirit, thus his lower drives were being sublimated.

When all the energies of the spirit are focused on Christ and His kingdom, sexual energies will not be eliminated, but they will be prevented from being a cause of frustration. Many single persons with a strong sex drive have found that it loses its persistent power when they lose themselves in strong service for the Master.

"The more a man denies himself, the more shall he obtain from God."

Horace Bushnell

Bible Verses to Help You

Therefore, I urge you, brothers, in view of God's mercy, to offer your bodies as living sacrifices, holy and pleasing to God – this is your spiritual act of worship.
(Romans 12:1)

Just as you used to offer the parts of your body in slavery to impurity and to ever-increasing wickedness, so now offer them in slavery to righteousness leading to holiness.
(Romans 6:19)

Suggested further reading

1 Corinthians 6:18–20

Reflect and respond

Are your motivations dominated by the flesh?

Have you placed sexual desire in proper context?

Place you energies in wholehearted devotion to God and His Kingdom.

36

When God's Promises are
Delayed

The Scriptures are full of instances of people struggling to make sense of God's delays. Take, for example, Abraham's long wait for a son. Or Joseph's extended years in prison as a victim of cruel circumstances. When something that God has promised is slow in coming to pass, life can become very confusing and perplexing. We look at opportunities that are being missed and cry out "Why? Why? Why?"

The first thing we should do when faced by a delayed promise is to check that we received a divine promise in the first place and that we are not victims of wishful thinking. Many take words from the Bible which were meant only for certain people in Scripture, apply them to themselves, and then become disappointed when they do not come to pass. So check to see that it was a clear promise God gave you from His Word.

Once you are sure of this then keep in mind that God brings things to pass at precisely the right time. There must be no equivocation on this point, for once we question the fact of God's perfect timing we open ourselves up to all kind of doubts. We can't stop doubt entering our heart, of course, but we can stop it lodging there. Whatever God has promised you (and you are sure it is a promise), then rest assured it will come to pass. Not always in your time. But always in His.

"Faith takes God without any ifs. If God says anything, faith says, "I believe it"; faith says, "Amen" to it."

D. L. Moody

Bible Verses to Help You

For he remembered his holy promise given to his servant Abraham
(Psalm 105:42)

Let us hold unswervingly to the hope we profess, for he who promised is faithful.
(Hebrews 10:23)

Suggested further reading

Habakkuk 2:1–3

Reflect and respond

Are questions over God's "timing" dominating your life?

Are your sure of God's promises to you?

Trust that the Father has your life in His faithful hands.

37

When Your Love for the Lord Begins to **Wane**

It should always cause us great concern when our love for the Lord Jesus Christ diminishes and wanes. Our love for Christ, we must always remember, is a response to His love for us. "We love because he first loved us," says the apostle John in 1 John 4:19. Our souls are designed to respond to divine love, not manufacture it. When we focus on how much we are loved by Him, and allow ourselves to be impacted by that fact, it will inevitably create a response in us. However, it must be emphasised that this principle will only work when sin has been put out of our hearts. In Revelation 2:4 our Lord says to the church in Ephesus: "I have this against you, that you have left your first love" (NKJ). Note they had not lost their love, but left it. There is a great difference between losing something and leaving it. We leave our love for Christ when we violate one or more of His commandments, and love cannot be recovered until sin is confessed and God's forgiveness sought.

Once all is dealt with then the principle mentioned above should be followed – focus not so much on how you can love Him but on His love for you. Gaze on the cross, see love bleeding for you. The greater your awareness of how much you are loved, the greater will be your response.

"I love, my God, but with no love of mine, For I have none to give; I love thee, Lord, but all the love is thine, For by thy love I live."

Jeanne Marie de la Mothe Guyon

Bible Verses to Help You

How great is the love the Father has lavished on us, that we should be called children of God! And that is what we are! (1 John 3:1)

What, then, shall we say in response to this? If God is for us, who can be against us? He who did not spare his own Son, but gave him up for us all – how will he not also, along with him, graciously give us all things? (Romans 8:31–32)

Suggested further reading

Ephesians 3:17–19

Reflect and respond

Identify any areas of your life that have cooled between God and you.

Look to the cross afresh, and meditate on His love for you.

38

When Marriage
Fails

The break-up of a marriage can be more traumatic and painful than even the death of
one's partner. In death one says "goodbye", and
after a period of grief and mourning the heart
gathers new strength and feels alive once again.
But a separation or divorce takes a toll that is
hard to describe. Friends can help and be a great
support, but there is no one who understands
like Jesus. He knows, more than anyone, what it
means to be rejected, misunderstood, and hurt.

First we must talk to God about the matter. It
is vitally important to acknowledge to yourself
and to God all your hurt or angry feelings. Next,
search the Scriptures daily, asking God to give
you words of encouragement. God quickens different Scriptures to different people. The Psalms
can be of special help in this connection, Third,
come to terms, painful though it may be, with the
fact your marriage may not be restored. If there
is hope that it may then live in that hope, but also
in the knowledge that it may not.

Fourth, remind yourself that you are first a person before being a partner. Though a partnership may be broken your identity as a person in Christ cannot. Fifth, develop a close and continuing relationship with God in prayer. Being bereft of a partner brings a certain loneliness, but it provides an opportunity for knowing God in a way you might never have known Him before.

> *"Man is born broken. He lives by mending. The grace of God is glue."*
>
> Eugene Gladstone O'Neil

Bible verses to Help You

My soul finds rest in God alone; my salvation comes from him. He alone is my rock and my salvation; he is my fortress, I shall never be shaken.
(Psalm 62:1–2)

The Lord is faithful to all his promises and loving towards all he has made. The Lord upholds all those who fall and lifts up all who are bowed down.
(Psalm 145:13–14)

Suggested further reading

Nehemiah 1:4 and Matthew 6:15

Reflect and respond

Is Jesus at the centre of your pain?

Have you talked over with God how you feel?

See this as an opportunity to draw closer to the Father.

39

When Someone Close to You
Dies

Sooner or later almost every one of us has to
face the death of a person we love. Forgive the
personal reference here, but some years ago I lost
my wife through cancer and I know what I am
about to say is true.

When death takes from our side someone we
love, the pain we experience can, at times, be
almost intolerable. We must not be afraid to
express our feelings to God whatever they may
be – anger, frustration, fear, hurt, and so on.
These feelings are better expressed than
repressed. C. S. Lewis said that when his wife
died he railed against God for a while. Then,
when he had spent himself in accusations
against the Almighty, He sensed the loving arms
of God go around Him in a way that even he was
unable to describe. God is not upset with us
when we tell Him exactly how we feel, He listens,
feels for us, and understands. As soon as
possible, though, we must invite Him into our
pain and draw upon His comforting strength
and support.

Divine comfort does not mean that our tears will dry up, or our grief come to a sudden halt. These are natural processes that have a powerful therapeutic effect. What it does mean is that we will feel God there in the midst of our tears and grief. The pain must be entered into and worked through – even the pain of saying ... goodbye.

"To weep is to make less the depth of grief."
William Shakespeare

Bible Verses to Help You

Blessed are those who mourn, for they will be comforted.
(Matthew 5:4)

Remember your word to your servant, for you have given me hope. My comfort in my suffering is this: Your promise preserves my life.
(Psalm 119:49–50)

Suggested further reading

Psalm 23:1–4

Reflect and respond

Have you acknowledged your pain to God?

Understand that the mourning process is healthy and needed.

Allow the tears to act as divine therapy – draw close to God.

40

When Sick and Tired of Being Sick and *Tired*

Clearly, the Scriptures reveal that God is able and willing to heal the sicknesses of His people. He healed men and women in Old Testament times, and in New Testament times too. When serious sickness afflicts us we ought to seek all legitimate means of healing, beginning first with inviting those who represent the local church to pray over us, anointing us with oil (James 5:14). Also, it is not lack of faith to seek medical help when sick – even when one has been prayed for by the leaders of the church.

But what happens when sickness continues and healing does not come? God is able to keep us brave when not blithe; aware of His presence even though not abounding with vitality. God does not always heal, and no matter how we may rationalise this fact we must see there is an element of mystery about the subject of healing. No one knew or has ever been more conscious of the problem of why God does not always deliver us from our afflictions than God's servant Job. He asked numerous questions of the Almighty but none of them, in fact, was answered. Instead God gave Job something better – a richer and deeper sense of His presence.

God may not give us a clear answer as to why we are not healed but He will, if we let Him, give us a richer awareness of Himself. Nothing can be more wonderful than that.

"God whispers to us in our pleasures, speaks in our conscience, but shouts in our pains: it is his megaphone to rouse a deaf world."

C.S. Lewis

Bible Verse to Help You

Praise the Lord, O my soul; all my inmost being, praise his holy name. Praise the Lord, O my soul, and forget not all his benefits – who forgives all your sins and heals all your diseases, who redeems your life from the pit and crowns you with love and compassion, who satisfies your desires with good things so that your youth is renewed like the eagle's.
(Psalm 103:1–5)

Suggested further reading

Matthew 8:16–17

Reflect and respond

Have you asked the leaders in your church to pray for you?

Have you taken the practical medical steps that are necessary?

Dig deep to feel the loving arms of the great Healer – Jesus.

Content Source Material

Sections 1, 3 and 5–7 are taken from:
Dr Bill & Frances Munro, *A Place of Rest*,
CWR, 1996.

Sections 2, 4, 16–18 and 20–40 are taken from:
Selwyn Hughes, *Your Personal Encourager*,
CWR, 1994.

Sections 10 and 14–15 are taken from:
Hilary Vogel, *Strength to Care*,
CWR, 1996.

Sections 8–9 and 19 are taken from:
David & Maureen Brown, *Breakthrough to Love*,
CWR, 1996.

Sections 11–13 are taken from:
Helena Wilkinson, *Doorway to Hope*,
CWR, 1995.

All these titles available from CWR
(see following pages for details).

National Distributors

UK: (and countries not listed below)
CWR, PO Box 230, Farnham, Surrey GU9 8XG.
Tel: (01252) 784710 Outside UK (44) 1252 784710

AUSTRALIA: CMC Australasia, PO Box 519, Belmont, Victoria 3216.
Tel: (03) 5241 3288

CANADA: CMC Distribution Ltd, PO Box 7000, Niagara on the Lake,
Ontario L0S 1J0.
Tel: (0800) 325 1297

GHANA: Challenge Enterprises of Ghana, PO Box 5723, Accra.
Tel: (021) 222437/223249 Fax: (021) 226227

HONG KONG: Cross Communications Ltd, 1/F, 562A Nathan Road,
Kowloon.
Tel: 2780 1188 Fax: 2770 6229

INDIA: Crystal Communications, 10-3-18/4/1, East Marredpally,
Secunderabad – 500 026.
Tel/Fax: (040) 7732801

KENYA: Keswick Bookshop, PO Box 10242, Nairobi.
Tel: (02) 331692/226047

MALAYSIA: Salvation Book Centre (M) Sdn Bhd, 23 Jalan SS 2/64,
47300 Petaling Jaya, Selangor.
Tel: (03) 78766411/78766797
Fax: (03) 78757066/78756360

NEW ZEALAND: CMC New Zealand Ltd, Private Bag,
17910 Green Lane, Auckland.
Tel: (09) 5249393 Fax: (09) 5222137

NIGERIA: FBFM, Helen Baugh House, 96 St Finbarr's College Road,

Akoka, Lagos.
Tel: (01) 7747429/4700218/825775/827264

PHILIPPINES: OMF Literature Inc, 776 Boni Avenue, Mandaluyong City.
Tel: (02) 531 2183 Fax: (02) 531 1960

REPUBLIC OF IRELAND: Scripture Union, 40 Talbot Street, Dublin 1.
Tel: (01) 8363764

SINGAPORE: Campus Crusade Asia Ltd, 315 Outram Road, 06-08 Tan
Boon Liat Building, Singapore 169074.
Tel: (065) 222 3640

SOUTH AFRICA: Struik Christian Books, 80 MacKenzie Street, PO Box
1144, Cape Town 8000.
Tel: (021) 462 4360 Fax: (021) 461 3612

SRI LANKA: Christombu Books, 27 Hospital Street, Colombo 1.
Tel: (01) 433142/328909

TANZANIA: CLC Christian Book Centre, PO Box 1384, Mkwepu Street,
Dar es Salaam.
Tel: (051) 2119439

UGANDA: New Day Bookshop, PO Box 2021, Kampala.
Tel: (041) 255377

ZIMBABWE: Word of Life Books, Shop 4, Memorial Building, 35 S Machel
Avenue, Harare.
Tel: (04) 781305 Fax: (04) 774739

For e-mail addresses, visit the CWR web site: www.cwr.org.uk

ISBN 1 85345 1789

ISBN 1 85345 1797

ISBN 1 85345 1770

ISBN 1 85345 1800

This new *Pocket Encourager* series offers biblical help, guidance and encouragement for everyone. Each title explores various aspects of the Christian experience, such as relationships, Bible study and coping with responsibility. Great gifts!

£3.99 each

Cover to Cover and *Cover to Cover – God's People* are exciting annual reading plans available in 6 partworks with their own attractive case, or as a softback book. *Cover to Cover* is now also available in hardback.

Cover to Cover

Cover to Cover explores God's Word chronologically, taking in the events of history as they happened with charts, maps, illustrations, diagrams and a helpful time line that places the Bible in a historical context.

Cover to Cover – God's People

Cover to Cover – God's People profiles 58 of the Bible's most fascinating and instructive personalities, helping you to learn invaluable lessons from these men and women of Scripture.

Softback and partworks	**£9.95**
Cover to Cover hardback	**£12.95**

These inspiring devotionals contain six, specially selected themes from *Every Day with Jesus* that will nourish your soul and stimulate your faith. Each book contains 365 undated daily readings, prayers, further study questions and a topical index.

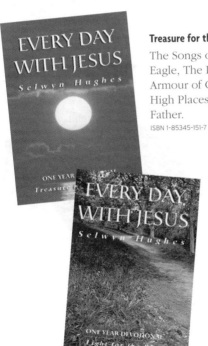

Treasure for the Heart

The Songs of Ascents, The Divine Eagle, The Lord's Prayer, The Armour of God, Hind's Feet on High Places, Your Father and My Father.

ISBN 1-85345-151-7

Light for the Path

The Uniqueness of our Faith, The Search for Meaning, The Twenty-third Psalm, The Spirit-filled Life, Strong at the Broken Places, Going Deeper with God.

ISBN 1-85345-134-7

A Fresh Vision of God

The Vision of God, From Confusion to
Confidence, The Beatitudes, The Power of a New
Perspective, The Corn of Wheat Afraid to Die,
Heaven-sent Revival.
ISBN 1-85345-121-5

Water for the Soul

Staying Spiritually Fresh,
Rebuilding Broken Walls,
The Character of God,
When Sovereignty Surprises,
The Fruit of the Spirit,
Seven Pillars of Wisdom.
ISBN 1-85345-128-2

£5.99 each

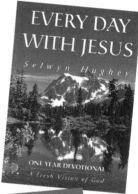

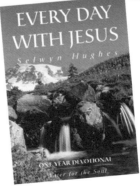

What would Christ have to say about our modern-day problems?
"He would give the same answers that He gave us in His Word",
says *Every Day with Jesus* author, Selwyn Hughes.

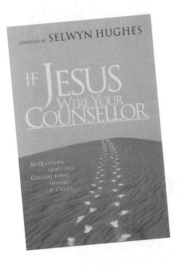

£6.95

Softback, 280 pages
198 x 130mm

If Jesus were your Counsellor
offers 50 biblical answers to
questions about faith and life.
Selwyn Hughes brings more
than four decades of counselling experience to this easy
to follow and beautifully
designed book, which recog-
nises that Scripture always
holds the answer.

*If Jesus were your
Counsellor* uses *The Message*
translation of the New
Testament, making it contem-
porary and easy to understand,
and the book-mark extensions
to the cover provide a simple
and effective way to keep your
place as you read Christ's
response
to issues such as love,
loneliness, relationships,
guilt and belief.

Let Jesus be your Counsellor.

The Discipleship Series combines practical advice with biblical principles to bring you invaluable insights into your faith in Jesus and growing with Him. Each title considers some of the most vital aspects of Christian living, such as marriage, prayer, and the Church. Essential reading!

10 Principles for a Happy Marriage

- Engaging approach to marriage God's way
- Healthy marriage check list
- Practical advice and help

15 Ways to a More Effective Prayer Life

- Revolutionise your prayer life
- Flexible suggestions for the individual
- Considers different personalities and lifestyles

5 Insights to Discovering Your Place in the Body of Christ

- Understanding the gifts in Scripture
- Discovering your ministry
- Developing your gift

£3.95 each